Copyright 2023

Table of Contents

PREVIEW

A disorder that affects a person's ability to think, feel and behave clearly.

The exact cause of schizophrenia isn't known, but a combination of genetics, environment and altered brain chemistry and structure may play a role.

Schizophrenia is characterised by thoughts or experiences that seem out of touch with reality, disorganised speech or behaviour and decreased participation in daily activities. Difficulty with concentration and memory may also be present.

Treatment is usually lifelong and often involves a combination of medications, psychotherapy and coordinated speciality care services.

Schizophrenia is a chronic, severe mental disorder that affects the way a person thinks, acts, expresses emotions, perceives reality, and relates to others. Though schizophrenia isn't as common as other major mental illnesses, it can be the most chronic and disabling.

People with schizophrenia often have problems doing well in society, at work, at school, and in relationships. They might feel frightened and withdrawn, and could appear to have lost touch with reality. This lifelong disease can't be cured but can be controlled with proper treatment.

Contrary to popular belief, schizophrenia is not a split or multiple personality. Schizophrenia involves a psychosis, a type of mental illness in which a person can't tell what's real from what's imagined. At times, people with psychotic disorders lose touch with reality. The world may seem like a jumble of confusing thoughts, images, and sounds. Their behaviour may be very strange and even shocking. A sudden change in personality and behaviour, which happens when people who have it lose touch with reality, is called a psychotic episode.

The symptoms of schizophrenia usually appear in late adolescence or early adulthood. Schizophrenia can affect a person's speech, thinking, emotions as well as social interactions and other everyday activities.

SCHIZOPHRENIA DIET RECIPES

BREAKFAST

1. Macro-Friendlier Scotch Eggs

Prep Time: 30 Minutes

Cook Time: 40 Minutes

Servings: 4

Ingredients

- 1 container (16oz) Hot Turkey Breakfast Sausage
- 1 egg, beaten (you won't use the whole thing for macro purposes)
- 4 eggs, hardboiled & peeled
- 1-2 cups breadcrumbs (you won't use all of this, but you need a lot to "roll" the sausage in)

Instructions

1. Hard boil your eggs however you want. I am always the person that googles how to do this every time. I suggest letting them chill for a while in the fridge so maybe do this the day before

2. Peel your eggs. This is my least favorite step.

3. Preheat your oven to 400 degrees F

4. Divide the sausage into 4 equal parts (4 oz each) and wrap each egg in sausage. The easiest way to do this is to flatten the sausage into a round disk, then wrap the egg in it & smooth it over until the egg is completely covered.

5. Once all eggs are covered take one egg & place it in a small bowl & beat it to mix. Measure the entire bowl + egg if you are curious to see how much egg you use.

6. Then take another bowl and dump in quite a bit of bread crumbs—remember you won't use it all, but you do need to have a lot of crumbs in the bowl so that its easy to coat the scotch eggs. Weigh the entire bowl + breadcrumbs if you are curious to see the exact amount of breadcrumbs you use.

7. Prepare your baking sheet/pan. I usually spray a 9×13 pan.

8. Now take one sausage/egg ball and roll it first in the beaten egg, then roll it in the breadcrumbs until it is completely coated. Place in the baking dish.

9. Repeat until all eggs are covered. (Now you can weigh your egg bowl & breadcrumb bowl again to find the difference which is the amount that was used)

10. Bake for ~35 minutes until the sausage is fully cooked/ no longer pink.

11. Eat right away OR let cool, then wrap individually in foil to grab out of the fridge & microwave when needed. (I cut mine in half & microwave on a plate for like 10 seconds)

2. Sausage, Egg, & Cheese "McMuffin"

Prep Time: 10 Minutes

Cook Time: 20 Minutes

Servings: 1

Ingredients

- 1, 100 cal Thomases Multi-grain English muffin
- 3oz turkey sausage
- 50ml egg whites
- 1 velveeta cheddar slice

Instructions

1. Get yourself a tiny pan, i got mine for $5 at the grocery store.
2. Spray the pan and pour your egg whites in. Add salt and garlic
3. Spray another pan and smash your turkey sausage as thin as you can get it because it will shrink up then it cools before putting it in the pan
4. Make sure to flip the sausage patty a few times
5. When everything is mostly cooked, cut English muffin and a half and toast it
6. Assemble your sandwich
7. Served with a side of fruit or oats for more carbs

3. Beef, Bloobs, & Brown Sugar Cinnamon Cream of Rice

Prep Time: 20 Minutes

Cook Time: 20 Minutes

Servings: 1

Ingredients

- 34g @thepridefoods Brown sugar cinnamon Cream Of rice
- 3oz 96/4 beef, weighed raw
- 50g frozen wild blueberries
- Walden farms pancake syrup
- Seasonings
- Onion powder
- Cinnamon
- Garlic powder
- Paprika
- Sea salt
- Just a bit of cayenne pepper and red pepper flakes

Instructions

1. Season the beef, yes with cinnamon to, and cook in a sprayed pan
2. Once the meat has browned, add your blueberries and a dash of pancake syrup
3. Let it simmer while you prep the cream of rice
4. Prep cream of rice according to the package directions. I did the microwave to save time. I added a dash of extra cinnamon too
5. Stir cream of rice and then top with beef and blueberries
6. Sprinkle extra cinnamon on top and then add more pancake syrup
7. Weird out everyone around you! And enjoy

4. Pumpkin Cheesecake Cauli Oats

Prep Time: 15 Minutes

Cook Time: 15 Minutes

Servings: 1

Ingredients

- 100g frozen cauli rice
- 100g canned pumpkin
- 40-60ml @skinnymixes syrup to sweeten
- 6g Jello cheesecake sugar free pudding mix
- 3/4 tsp pumpkin pie spice
- A dash of cinnamon and vanilla
- Water- just enough to make the mi100-200g egg whites
- Toppings
- Nut Butter- this one is pumpkin cheesecake
- More cinnamon
- Walden farms pancake syrup

Instructions

1. Microwave or frozen cauliflower for 60 to 90 seconds until warm
2. Place a cauliflower, pumpkin, skinny syrup, spices, water and extracts to a bowl. Use an immersion blender to blend everything together until there are no more chunks of cauliflower
3. Transfer everything to a pot, add the packet of oats and mix and see if you need more water, if it's thick add more water
4. Using a whisk, heat on the stove top, stirring continuously until the oats have thickened
5. Add your egg whites, stir continuously to avoid clumps and cook until thickened again
6. Remove from the heat, place in another bowl and add your toppings

5. Loaded Baked Potato Cream of Rice

Prep Time: 15 Minutes

Cook Time: 15 Minutes

Servings: 1

Ingredients

- 32g+ @thepridefoods UNFLAVORED cream of rice
- 80-130g egg whites, choose depending on your needs, i do 80 normally
- 20g spinach
- 3 sliced deli ham
- 15g velveeta cheddar shreds
- Salt, garlic, hella seasoning

Instructions

1. Place cream of rice plus seasonings into a pot and add water according to the package directions. Do not skimp on the salt, its bland rice and it needs some flavor add garlic powder also
2. Cook according to the package directions, stirring frequently

3. In a separate pan sauté your deli ham to crisp it up, essentially pretend it's bacon and sauté your spinach

4. When the cream of rice is thickened, stir in your egg whites

5. Let cook until thickened again dumpster and your cheese and sautéed ham

6. Mediterranean Ham & Veggie Breakfast Crunch Wrap

Prep Time: 15 Minutes

Cook Time: 15 Minutes

Servings: 1

Ingredients

- 1 @cutdacarb or Joseph's Lavash Wrap
- 1 laughing cow lite Swiss cheese
- Rosemary (fresh is preferred)
- 60g Deli Sliced Ham
- Hummus (i used Mediterranean olive flavor)
- 80g egg whites
- 15g light mozzarella shredded cheese
- 50g dices bell pepper
- 3oz baby Bella mushrooms
- Other seasonings, salt, garlic powder, onion powder etc

Instructions

1. In the smallest pan you have, cook your egg whites (you want them to be a small circular shape to fit in your

crunch wrap) I usually sprinkle the edd whites with garlic powder/salt then cover with pan while they cook.

2. Cook your mushrooms and bell pepper. I cooked them separately, buy you could cook them together! Season them here.

3. Lay out your wrap, spread the laughing cow cheese in a circle in the middle

4. Lay your ham on top of the cheese and sprinkle with rosemary.

5. Place your egg white circle on top of the ham then top with hummus, peppers, mozzarella and mushrooms

6. Carefully fold up your wrap. Then spray with oil and place into the air fryer seam side down. Or you can do this in a pan.

7. Cook until golden brown on both sides. – 5 minutes in the air fryer, in a pan it's about the same per side.

8. Cut in half and enjoy!

7. Low Calorie French toast

Prep Time: 25 Minutes

Cook Time: 20 Minutes

Servings: 1

Ingredients

- 2 slices of bread (I used Nature's own 40 calorie Honey Wheat)
- 40ml Almond Milk
- 40g egg whites
- 20g Walden farms sugar free syrup
- Cinnamon- optional
- Topping Ideas
- Swerve powdered sugar
- More pancake syrup
- Bloobs
- Nut butter
- Powdered nut butter

Instructions

1. Combined milk, egg whites, pancake syrup, and cinnamon in a bowl
2. Heat a large pan
3. So each slice of bread in the mixture
4. Spray the pan and fry up your French toast bread until its brown on both sides
5. Serve with whatever toppings your heart desires and a side of extra protein like eggs for a complete breakfast

8. Banana Protein Pancakes

Prep Time: 60 Minutes

Cook Time: 15 Minutes

Servings: 1

Ingredients

- 1 banana
- 140g egg whites
- 1.5 tsp @pamelasproducts not can thin not guar
- 1.5 tsp baking powder
- 5g psyllium husk
- Cinnamon
- 7g nestle mini chocolate chips
- Stevia Sweetener i used 10g of a skinny syrup

Instructions

1. In a measuring cup, mash the banana
2. Add egg whites, start to combine
3. In a separate small bowl, combine the dry ingredients

4. I have the dry ingredients to the way. Are used an immersion blender because I found that stirring by hand is not enough to eliminate clumps

5. Let the batter set a minimum of 20 minutes. Anywhere from 20 to 60 is good. This will let the batter thicken up don't skip this

6. On a preheated pan, cook your pancakes. They will take a while to cook on each side and you know they are ready to be flipped when they pop up and bubble start to form. Again, be patient with it

7. Serve with pancake syrup

9. Pumpkin Chocolate Chip Protein Muffins

Prep Time: 15 Minutes

Cook Time: 30 Minutes

Servings: 8

Ingredients

- 180g canned pumpkin
- 60ml @skinnymixes liquid sweetener
- 100ml egg whites
- 1/4-1/3 cup water
- 15ml vegetable/coconut oil
- 40g unsweetened applesauce
- 1/2 tsp vanilla extract
- 60g @pescience vegan cinnamon delight protein powder
- 40g all-purpose flour
- 1/2 tsp baking powder
- 1/2 tsp baking soda
- 1/2 tsp salt
- 28g nestle mini chocolate chips

Instructions

1. Preheat oven to 400
2. Mix wet ingredients together, then the dry, and then add chocolate chips
3. Divide batter into 8 liners in a muffin tin, back for 20-25 minutes
4. Insert a tooth pick, when it comes out clean they are done

10. Peanut Butter Cauliflower Oats

Prep Time: 15 Minutes

Cook Time: 10 Minutes

Servings: 1

Ingredients

- 40g quick oats
- 16g riced cauliflower
- Skinny syrup to taste
- Vanilla extract
- 200g egg whites
- 10g PB2
- TOppings
- 1 banana
- 2tbsp chocolate almond bar PB powder

Instructions

1. Microwave your frozen cauliflower for 60 to 90 seconds until warm

2. Please oats in a small pot with cauliflower 40 to 60 g skinny syrup vanilla extract and just enough water to cover the oats

3. Using a whisk on the stove top stirring continuously until the oats have thickened

4. Add your egg whites

5. Stir continuously to avoid clumps and cook until thickened again

6. Remove from heat and stir in in the dry mix peanut butter powder

7. Place in another bowl and add your toppings

LUNCH

11. Mexican Sweet Potato Skillet

Prep Time: 15 Minutes

Cook Time: 40 Minutes

Servings: 4

Ingredients

- 16oz (1lb) ground chicken
- Diced Bell Pepper (I buy the pre-diced kind, mine came out to 195g) ~2 peppers would work here!
- 1-2 garlic cloves (or 1 tbsp if you just use the pre diced stuff from the grocery like me)
- 1 large sweet potato, large diced. (Mine came out to 340g) (Or two smaller sweet potatoes)
- 1 can of pinto beans (mine weighed 264g after draining)
- 1 can fire roasted rotel tomatoes with green chilies
- 100g Velveeta Cheddar Shreds
- Chili Powder, Cumin, Salt, Pepper
- Cilantro (to garnish)

Instructions

1. Spray a large skillet with non-stick cooking spray and cook your ground chicken. Add 1 tbsp chili powder & 1 tsp of cumin + salt & pepper

2. Add the garlic, onion, & bell peppers once the chicken is mostly cooked & let cook 3-5 minutes

3. When the chicken is cooked, set aside in a bowl & wipe/wash the skillet (OR if you have a giant pot you can keep it all together, like an instant pot for example)

4. Combine the diced sweet potato, pinto beans, rotel tomatoes, & an additional 2 tsp chili powder + 1 tsp cumin + salt & pepper

5. Stir together, cover with a lid, & let simmer for 15-20 minutes until the sweet potato is soft (the larger your chunks of sweet potato the longer this will take)

6. Add the ground chicken mixture back to the skillet & stir it all together!

7. Top with cheese & cilantro it's ready to serve or be split into meal prep containers.

12. Fluffy Pancake Hack

Prep Time: 15 Minutes

Cook Time: 10 Minutes

Servings: 1

Ingredients

- 46g egg whites
- 10g nestle mini chocolate chips
- Water

Instructions

1. Using an electric mixer, whip your egg whites until they form fluffy peaks, i was aiming for stiff peaks, but got impatient after 5 minutes or so and you can see the last pictures I need up with softer peaks but even when i held the whisk upside down it didnt fall!
2. Measure out your pancake mix into a separate bowl and pour a small amount of water in it so that you can JUST mix them. I used 25ml of water and then mixed, it was VERY thick.

3. Gently fold in the beaten egg whites until combined. Do this with a spoon so you don't over mix.

4. Add your chocolate chips here, reserving a few to top your pancakes

5. Cook them in a tiny pan. I covered my baby frying pan with a lid and times it to 4 minutes when i was easily able to flip the pancakes

6. Serve with Walden Farms Pancake syrup

13. Whataburger Copycat Sausage, Egg, & Cheese Taquito

Prep Time: 20 Minutes

Cook Time: 12 Minutes

Servings: 1

Ingredients

- 1 Wrap of your choice (cutdacarb or lavash)
- 2oz hot turkey sausage
- 6oz egg whites
- 25g Velveeta Mexican Shreds
- 15g Tostitos Medium Salsa con Queso
- 1 whataburger picante sauce packet or another salsa of your choice

Instructions

1. Preheat oven to 450
2. Cook turkey sausage
3. To the same pan add egg whites and scramble. Add half the cheese and mix
4. While eggs are cooking lay out your wrap and spread the queso on one side

5. Carefully out your scrambled egg mixture on top of the wrap keeping it in one area

6. Fold the ends in and then wrap it up, spray cooking spray on a baking sheet and place the burrito there

7. Bake for 10-12 minutes, ENJOY!!

14. Migas

Prep Time: 20 Minutes

Cook Time: 15 Minutes

Servings: 1

Ingredients

- 3 mission extra thin corn tortilla
- 45g bell pepper, diced
- 6oz egg whites
- 85g chicken (not very Tex mex but i needed more protein)
- 15g velvets Mexican shreds
- 60g (2 servings) green salsa
- 80g black beans
- Spices- S&P, garlic, cumin, etc

Instructions

1. Slice your tortillas into thin strips and toss into a sprayed pan to crisp up, there is no surcharge thing as Too crisp for this recipe since they'll soften up when you add the egg

2. After a few minuted toss in the diced bell pepper

3. While that cooks, spread out your black beans in your serving bowl and microwave for 1-2 minutes

4. Once those have Cooke's, toss in your egg whites and spices

5. When your eggs are mostly cooked add in the salad and cheese shreds, continue cooking just long enough for it to all blend together.

6. Serve them on top of the beans and top with more cheese and salsa if you want

15. Chicken with Sauce Vierge, Saffron Couscous, & Asparagus

Prep Time: 20 Minutes

Cook Time: 20 Minutes

Servings: 5

Ingredients

- 16 oz Chicken Breast (or more)
- 2 cups of dry white rice
- Fresh Asparagus (I had 370g total)
- 1.5 cups chicken stock
- Saffron (1-2 pinches)
- For the sauce
- 250g green grapes
- 250g cherry tomatoes
- 1-2 cloves of garlic crushed, then minced
- 1 small shallot, minced
- 3 tbsp Italian parsley, chopped fine
- 1 tbsp tarragon, chopped fine
- 3.5 tbsp extra virgin olive oil (a NICE kind)
- Salt & pepper to taste (at LEAST 1 tbsp salt)
- 1-2 tbsp lemon juice
- 1-2 tbsp lime juice

Instructions

1. Bring the chicken stock to a simmer & add your saffron. Simmer for 5-10 minutes to allow it to bloom & release flavor.
2. Add the chicken stock to the dry rice & add any additional water needed. Cook the rice as instructed.
3. For the sauce, cut all of the grapes & tomatoes in half.
4. Add the grapes & tomatoes to a bowl with all the other ingredients for the sauce, then toss to combine
5. Taste & add more salt if needed (use GOOD salt here!)
6. Cook your chicken however you prefer—I seasoned mine with Ras Al Hanout seasoning & salt (again you can season however you'd like, it'll be delicious) & cooked it in a pan. I flipped it after 1 minute & then covered the pan & cooked on medium low for ~5 minutes until cooked through & it comes out SO JUICY!!
7. For the asparagus, bring a large pan of water to a simmer & add the asparagus. Cook for 2-4 minutes until the asparagus has turned a deeper green color. Remove from heat & plunge in an ice path to stop it from cooking further. Easy peasy.
8. To serve... put that sauce over everything!! (For macro purposes I divided the sauce evenly but do NOT put the

sauce into your meal prep containers already. We don't want the sauce to heat up in the microwave) this is a COLD sauce.

16. Apple Pie Cauli Oats

Prep Time: 15 Minutes

Cook Time: 20 Minutes

Servings: 1

Ingredients

- 1 packet @betteroats Apple Cinnamon 100 calorie packet
- 160g frozen cauliflower rice
- Lots of cinnamon, use your heart here
- 1/2 tsp caramel extract
- 200g water
- @skinnymixes skinny syrup to taste about 40-60g
- 200g egg whites, really you can do any amount you want here, but anything below 100g is not as creamy
- Toppings
- Nut butter~ this one has 28g Big apple from @americandreamnutbutter
- More cinnamon
- Walden farms pancake syrup

Instructions

1. Microwave your frozen cauliflower you for 60-90 seconds
2. Please oh packet in a small pot with cauliflower, 40 to 60 g skinny syrup, caramel extract, cinnamon and just enough water to cover the oats
3. Using a whisk, heat on the stove top, stirring continuously until the oats have a thickened
4. Add your egg whites
5. Stir continuously to avoid clumps and cook until thickened again
6. Place in another bowl and add your toppings

17. Blueberry Lemon Cauliflower Oats

Prep Time: 15 Minutes

Cook Time: 15 Minutes

Servings: 1

Ingredients

- 40g oats (any kind work)
- 120g frozen cauliflower rice
- 200g water
- 40-60g skinny syrup of choice
- A dash of cake batter extract
- 110g egg whites OR MORE if you want, i normally do about 200g
- 12g @flavoredpbco Blueberry cobbler peanut butter powder
- Toppings
- Frozen/fresh fruit 30g
- 20g squeeze the day lemon almond butter from @americandreamnutbutter

Instructions

1. Microwave your frozen cauliflower for 60 to 90 seconds until warm
2. Please let oats in a small pot with cauliflower, 40 to 60 g skinny syrup, cake batter extract and just enough water to cover the oats
3. Using a whisk, he on the stove top, stirring continuously until the oats up thickened
4. At your egg whites
5. Stir continuously to avoid clumps and cook until thickened again
6. Remove from heat and stir in in the blueberry cobbler peanut butter powder
7. Please in another bowl and add your toppings

18. Blueberry Cream Cheese Protein Muffins

Prep Time: 15 Minutes

Cook Time: 20 Minutes

Servings: 9

Ingredients

- 120g @pamcakespancakes Butter Milk protein pancake mic
- 20g @pescience vanilla protein powder
- 2g baking powder
- 1/2 tsp vanilla extract
- 1 container fat Free Cream Cheese
- 1 egg
- 46g egg whites
- 28g light canola butter
- 30-50 ml skinned syrup, or another sweetener of your choice
- 80g blueberries

Instructions

1. Set out your cream cheese/egg and let come to room temperature this is important or else your cream cheese will be too hard to mix
2. Preheat oven to 350
3. Cream Together the cheese, egg, egg whites, vanilla and butter
4. Add your pancake mix, protein powder and baking powder and MIX
5. I added my sweetener here. Since i used skinny syrup it helped with the needed liquid, if you use a powdered sweetener you will want to add a little almond milk
6. Gently fold in blueberries
7. Divide evenly into a parchment lined muffin tin. I got 9 out of this
8. Bake for 15-20 minutes or until the edges start to turn brown

19. Monster Cookie Peanut Butter Banana Bread

Prep Time: 30 Minutes

Cook Time: 25 Minutes

Servings: 9

Ingredients

- 2 ripe bananas
- 60g butter my cookie, or monster cookie peanut butter from @americandreamnutbutter
- 6tbsp egg whites
- 21g coconut flour
- 32g @pescience peanut butter cookie protein
- 15g cake flour or all purpose
- 4g baking powder
- 2-6g stevia
- 25g mini m&m's

Instructions

1. Preheat your oven to 350°
2. Mash your bananas

3. Add the wet ingredients, then your dry, and mix together

4. Add your mini M&Ms here and reserve some for toppings

5. Put into a sprayed muffin tin

6. Bake for about 20 to 25 minutes until you can insert a toothpick and it comes out clean

7. Store in fridge

20. Personal Peanut Butter Protein Banana Bread

Prep Time: 20 Minutes

Cook Time: 20 Minutes

Servings: 1

Ingredients

- 1/2 of a banana (50-60g)
- 20g nut butter of your choice
- 30 ml egg whites
- 1tbsp (7g) coconut flour
- 10g protein powder (a whey casein blend is preferable) I've tried it with both vanilla and @pescience cake pop
- 5g cake flour (all-purpose works too)
- 2g or 1/2 tsp baking powder
- Optional mini chocolate chips.sprinkles/etc for topping

Instructions

1. Preheat oven to 350
2. Mash your banana

3. Add the wet ingredients then your dry, mix together (add toppings here)

4. Put into sprayed mini loaf pan

5. Bake for 15-20 minutes until an inserted toothpick comes out clean!

DINNER

21. Buttermilk Protein Scones

Prep Time: 30 Minutes

Cook Time: 20 Minutes

Servings: 1

Ingredients

- 37g/1serving @pamcakespancakes Classic buttermilk pancake mix (code-me yogi fit)
- 10g all-purpose flour
- 1g or 1/2 tsp baking powder
- 1-2g stevia (about a packet and a half)
- 40g non-fat Greek yogurt
- 5g light Butter (Do Not Melt)
- 7g mini chocolate chips

Instructions

1. Preheat oven to 350 and link baking sheet with parchment paper
2. Mix all your dry ingredients together in a small bowl

3. Add your Greek yogurt and gently stir until its 80% mixed. The secret to scones is NOT over mixing, less is more here

4. Butter. IF you have the time FREEZE your butter over night. Otherwise measure out your 5g in a separate dish and then cut it up with a spoon into small chunks before adding it to your batter.

5. Mix. But Not Too Much. Butter chunks are good!

6. Add chocolate chips. (Or blueberries, yum)

7. Drop onto parchment paper lined pan. I used the spoon to shape it into a triangle.

8. Bake for 10-15 minutes until it starts to turn golden

22. Blueberry Lemon Protein Banana Bread

Prep Time: 15 Minutes

Cook Time: 25 Minutes

Servings: 1

Ingredients

- 1/2 large banana (60g)
- 20g Blueberry Muffin Almond butter
- 1tsp vanilla extract
- 1tbsp (7g) coconut flour
- 10g @pescience Cake Pop protein powder
- 5g cake flour
- 2g baking powder
- 3g lemon zest
- Squeeze of lemon juice
- 15-20g frozen blueberries

Instructions

1. Preheat oven 350
2. Mash your banana and zest the lemon
3. Add wet ingredients, then your dry, mix together

4. Put into a sprayed, mini loaf pan

5. Bake 20-25 minuted until inserted toothpick comes out
    clean!

23. Monte Cristo Crunch Wrap

Prep Time: 15 Minutes

Cook Time: 15 Minutes

Servings: 1

Ingredients

- 1 @cutdacarb wrap
- 1.5 slices of bread (i used nature's own 40 cal)
- 1oz milk (macros are for skim, you can. Use almond or whatever)
- 30g egg whites
- 1 laughing cow lite Swiss cheese
- 80g Black Forest ham (or however much you want)
- 30g+ Walden farms sugar free pancake syrup
- Cinnamon
- Optional: swerve powdered sugar for dusting

Instructions

1. Combined milk, egg whites, pancake syrup and cinnamon in a bowl

2. Cut your bread up into squares and let's soak for a few minutes in the liquid milk/egg white mixture

3. Honey lightly sprayed pan, fry up your French toast bread until it's browned on both sides

4. Lay your wrap out

5. Spread out one laughing cow light swish cheese in a circle in the middle. Keep it pretty narrow so you can fold everything in

6. Place your ham in the middle of the wrap on top of the cheese. Top with French toast and drizzle with some extra pancake syrup here

7. Fold the ends in to wrap it up, then spray

8. Spray with cooking spray, then either air fry or place seem so down on a hot pan flipping after a few minutes

9. That's with powdered sugar, keep the syrup close by, and enjoy

24. Egg White Oatmeal

Prep Time: 15 Minutes

Cook Time: 15 Minutes

Servings: 1

Ingredients

- 40g Oats of any kind, you can choose the amount you want here, just change the macros
- Water
- @skinnymixes skinny syrup to taste 20-40g (any flavor is good, i am enjoying cookie dough right now)
- Cake batter extract
- 100-200g egg whites- macros are for 100g
- 10g PB2 (can replace this with protein powder if you like)
- Toppings
- Nut butter! This one is 34g of Cupids Cloud Raspberry White Chocolate Almond Butter from @americandreamnutbuttter
- Frozen raspberries
- Other Ideas: mini chocolate chips, mini candies, pancake syrup

Instructions

1. Place oats in a small pot with 20 to 40 g skinny syrup, cake batter extract and just enough water to cover the oats
2. Using a whisk, heat on the stove top, stirring continuously until the oats have thickened
3. Add your egg whites
4. Start continuously to avoid clumps and cook until thickened again
5. Remove from heat and start in PB2 powder or protein powder of your choice
6. Place in another bowl and add your toppings

25. Mexican Sweet Potato Skillet

Prep Time: 15 Minutes

Cook Time: 40 Minutes

Servings: 4

Ingredients

- 16oz (1lb) 96/4 ground beef
- 30g Onion
- 1-2 garlic cloves (or 1 tbsp if you just use the pre diced stuff from the grocery like me)
- 1 large sweet potato, diced. (Mine came out to 385g) (Or two smaller sweet potatoes) 1 can of black beans (mine weighed 400g after draining)
- 1 can fire roasted rotel tomatoes & green chilies
- 112g Velveeta Cheddar Shreds
- Chili Powder, Cumin, Salt, Pepper
- Cilantro (to garnish)

Instructions

1. Spray a large skillet with non-stick cooking spray & cook your ground beef & onion together. Add 1 tbsp chili powder & 1 tsp of cumin + salt & pepper
2. Add the garlic once the beef is mostly cooked
3. When the beef is cooked (brown!), set aside in a bowl & wipe/wash the skillet
4. Combine the diced sweet potato, black beans, rotel tomatoes, & an additional 2 tsp chili powder + 1 tsp cumin + salt & pepper
5. Stir together, cover with a lid, & let simmer for 15-20 minutes until the sweet potato is soft (the larger your chunks of sweet potato the longer this will take)
6. Add the ground beef mixture back to the skillet & stir it all together!
7. Top with cheese & it's ready to serve or be split into meal prep containers.

26. Ratatouille Inspired Chicken & Rice Meal Prep

Prep Time: 15 Minutes

Cook Time: 30 Minutes

Servings: 4

Ingredients

- 20oz + chicken breast
- 8oz can Hunt's Tomato Sauce
- 14.5oz can Diced Tomatoes
- 2 tbsp Herbes de Provence (spice blend you can find at your grocery!)
- 1 cup chicken stop OR 1 tbsp Bouillon Chicken Stock Base
- 30g Frozen Spinach PER cup of dry rice
- Dry Rice (amount you make is up to you based on serving size you need!)
- 2 medium zucchini (~400g)
- 2 medium yellow squash (~400g)
- Optional: 1 bay leaf, 2-4 whole cardamom pods

Instructions

1. Toss the chicken, tomato sauce, & diced tomatoes into your Instant Pot OR slow cooker
2. Add the herbes de provence as well as salt & pepper to taste
3. Set your instant pot to 12 minutes on manual (high pressure) OR on high for 1-2 hours with your slow cooker
4. Add the frozen spinach to a blender & add enough chicken stock needed to cook your rice (IE if you're cooking 1 cup of dry rice would need 1.5 cups chicken stock/water) Blend.
5. Wash your rice & then add the spinach/stock mixture to the pot. Add your bay leaf & cardamom pods if you'd like some epic extra flavor.
6. Now finish cooking the rice according to package instructions. Remove the bay leaf & cardamom before serving!
7. Dice your zucchini & squash & saute in a sprayed pan with salt & pepper until the squash is just soft enough to pierce easily with a fork
8. Shred the chicken when it's done cooking & you're ready to serve!

27. Salsa Chicken with Poblano & Tomatillo Rice

Prep Time: 10 Minutes

Cook Time: 30 Minutes

Servings: 5

Ingredients

- 1 jar of salsa (your choice)
- 1-2lbs of Chicken breast
- Pico de Gallo (for topping)
- For the Poblano & Tomatillo Rice
- 1-2 cups of dry white rice (however much you need for the week)
- 1 cup chicken stock OR 1 tbsp of bouillon (as shown in the video)
- 1 poblano pepper
- 2 tomatillos
- 1/2 a Yellow Onion
- 2-3tbsp fresh cilantro

Instructions

1. Place the salsa & chicken breast in your instant pot or slower cooker. I do 13 minutes on my instant pot–if you're using a slow cooker you'll need to let it cook on high for 4 hours or on low for 6-8 until the chicken shreds easily with a fork. Don't toss the salsa (let it sit in the fridge with the salsa if you're prepping it?)

2. For the rice: Cut the poblano pepper in half & place in a small pot on the stove along with the tomatillos, half an onion, & chicken stock. Bring to a simmer & let cook, covered, for 5-10 minutes

3. Cook your rice according to package instructions

4. Place the cooked poblano, onion, tomatillos in a blender OR use an immersion blender with a small amount of the reserved chicken stock (just enough to blend it, too much will dilute it)

5. Add your fresh cilantro & blend

6. Pour as much of this poblano & tomatillo sauce as you'd like into your cooked rice & stir (you don't have to use it all)

7. Serve with the chicken & add fresh pico de gallo as a topping!

28. Instant Pot Cheesy Chicken Burrito Bowl

Prep Time: 5 Minutes

Cook Time: 20 Minutes

Servings: 6

Ingredients

- 16oz ground chicken
- 60g diced yellow onion (1/4 cup)
- ~200g diced bell pepper (~2 peppers)
- 1/2 cup of white rice (uncooked)
- 1 can of black beans (455g)
- 1 can of Original Rotel
- 1 bag of frozen cauliflower rice (340g)
- 16oz jar of salsa of your choice (I used a cilantro kind that was 2c per tablespoon)
- 1 cup (8oz) chicken broth
- 56g Velveeta Mexican Shreds

Instructions

1. Using the saute function on the instant pot, use some spray oil & cook the ground chicken. Season to taste with salt/pepper.
2. Add the onion & bell pepper & cook for 3-5 more minutes.
3. Microwave the bag of cauliflower rice for ~2 minutes just to break up any big frozen chunks
4. Add all the rest of the ingredients to the instant pot & stir
5. Turn off the saute function & place the lid on the instant pot
6. Cook at high pressure for 7 minutes
7. Top with cheese before serving!

29. Miracle Noodle Pad Thai

Prep Time: 15 Minutes

Cook Time: 20 Minutes

Servings: 1

Ingredients

- 2 packages of miracle noodle fettuccine
- 85g broccoli (i used frozen and reheat it. Or use whatever veggie you want)
- 85g grilled chicken breast
- 1tbsp east-west Asian peanut sauce
- Sriracha (optional)

Instructions

1. Rinse the miracle noodles in a colander for a minute and then toss into a pot of boiling water for 1-2 minutes and then drain.
2. In a non-stick pan or a sprayed pan, cook noodles for 5-10 minutes. This will help dehydrate them and make them less chewy.

3. Add your veggies and chicken, cook until no longer frozen, then add your sauce

4. Spices I'd recommend: ginger, salt, garlic, onion powder etc.

5. Try not to burn your tongue

30. Grilled Cheese Tomato Soup Crunch Wrap

Prep Time: 15 Minutes

Cook Time: 45 Minutes

Servings: 1

Ingredients

- 1 wrap, i use @cutdacarb
- 60g raw cherry/grape/sweet tomatoes
- 20-30g velveeta cheddar shreds
- 3 oz deli sliced ham
- 30g spinach
- Salt, garlic powder

Instructions

1. Preheat your oven to 350° and line a baking sheet with foil for easy clean up
2. Wash your tiny tomatoes and then choose to either cut them in half or leave them whole, spray with olive oil spray and season with salt and garlic. Then placed on prepared tray

3. Bake tomatoes for about 30 minutes. I am recommend doing a large batch of these, then saving the rest for leftovers

4. I lay out your wrap and place the cheese in the middle, then add your roasted tomatoes and ham.

5. Pile your spinach on top, add a crack of salt

6. Carefully wrap it up.

7. Spray with cooking spray, then either air fry or place seems side down on a hot pan flipping after a few minutes

8. Cut in half and serve with a side of veggies, baby potatoes or even a bowl of tomato soup